2017 NACWE Prayer Call Handouts

2017 NACWE Prayer Call Handouts, Copyright 2017 by National Association of Christian Women Entrepreneurs (NACWE)

Scripture quotations marked (NIV) are taken from the Holy Bible, New International Version®, NIV®. Copyright © 1973, 1978, 1984, 2011 by Biblica, Inc.™ Used by permission of Zondervan. All rights reserved worldwide. www.zondervan.com The "NIV" and "New International Version" are trademarks registered in the United States Patent and Trademark Office by Biblica, Inc.™

Scripture quotations marked (ESV) are from The ESV® Bible (The Holy Bible, English Standard Version®), copyright © 2001 by Crossway, a publishing ministry of Good News Publishers. Used by permission. All rights reserved."

All NACWE prayer call handouts were inserted in their original format, which accounts for various inconsistencies throughout the book.

RHEMA Publishing House.
rhemapublishinghouse.com
PO Box 1244 McKinney, TX

ISBN: 978-0-9990932-5-2

Welcome to the Soul of NACWE!

The National Association of Christian Women Entrepreneurs (NACWE) has always been known for its heart, and we want to formally introduce you to our prayer and devotion corner, the Soul of NACWE. Our sisterhood is here to support you on your personal journey of faith and how that is intertwined with your business. We believe in the transforming power of prayer.

- **We pray daily for our Members**
- **We pray together weekly in a special Members call**
- **We hand out a weekly Prayer Call guide, and we offer these to you in this booklet.**

In our businesses, God is our CEO.

For Members of the National Association of Christian Women Entrepreneurs, Devotion to God comes first and we are reminded of the acrostic: **J - O - Y**

J stands for Jesus—He comes first.
O stands for others—they come next.
Y stands for yourself—and in this group, your Entrepreneurial endeavors!

Jesus First: *"But seek first the kingdom of God and his righteousness, and all these things will be added to you*.*"* Matthew 6:33

Others Next: *"As each has received a gift, use it to serve one another, as good stewards of God's varied grace..."* 1 Peter 4:10

Your Work: *"Commit your work to the Lord, and your plans will be established."* Proverbs 16:3

LEADERS AND MEMBERS IN NACWE ARE COMMITTED
AND DEDICATED TO GOD AND HIS WAYS.

Thank you to all who have led us in these endeavors by managing, leading, writing, and praying; you are SO dear to us!
  -Barbara Hollace, Sally Adamcik, Marian Struble, Diane Cunningham, Karen Lindwall- Bourg, and Courtenay Blackwell
  -and all participating NACWE Members

Prayer Calls 2017

Transformed	*1*
Respect	*2*
Willing	*3*
Endurance	*4*
Renew	*5*
Confidence	*6*
Devoted	*7*
Praise	*8*
Joy	*9*
Powerful	*10*
Surrender	*11*
Freedom	*12*
Healing	*13*
Words	*14*
Thoughts	*15*
Actions	*16*
Encourage	*17*
Honor	*18*
Celebrate	*19*
Presence	*20*
Serve	*21*
Protect	*22*
Anxiety/Anxious	*23*
Time	*24*
Comfort	*25*
Rejoice	*26*
Kindness	*27*
Humility	*28*
Support	*29*
Treasure	*30*

Appearance *31*
Declare. *32*
Compassion *33*
Mountains *34*
Knowledge *35*

Blessing *36*
Order *37*
Depend. *38*
Glory *39*

Believe *40*
Money *41*
Gratefulness. *42*
Stewardship. *43*

Notability. *44*
Rejoice *45*
Hope. *46*
Salvation/Rescue *47*

NACWE PRAYER CALL   January 5, 2017
TRANSFORMED

One of the characteristics that makes NACWE unique is we are the National Association of <u>Christian</u> Women Entrepreneurs. It's our first prayer call of 2017. God calls us to be transformed… that's not just a little adjustment, that's a <u>supernatural</u> change!

SCRIPTURE:

Do not conform to the pattern of this world, but be **transform**ed by the renewing of your mind. Then you will be able to test and approve what God's will is—His good, pleasing and perfect will. ~ **Romans 12:2 (NIV)**

But we all, with unveiled face, beholding as in a mirror the glory of the Lord, are being transformed into the same image from glory to glory, just as from the Lord, the Spirit.
~ **2 Corinthians 3:18 (NASB)**

Who, by the power that enables him to bring everything under his control, will **transform** our lowly bodies so that they will be like his glorious body.
~ **Philippians 3:21 (NIV)**

QUOTE: "My worldview, my philosophy, my attitudes, my relationships, my parenting, my marriage - everything has been transformed by my relationship with Christ." ~ **Lee Strobel**

DISCUSSION: In this first week of 2017, what is one area of your life that needs supernatural transformation (an attitude, a habit, a way of thinking, etc.)? What's one step you can take to make a change?

PRAYER: Open for prayer requests.

© 2016 National Association of Christian Women Entrepreneurs * All Rights Reserved * www.nacwe.org

NACWE PRAYER CALL   January 12, 2017
RESPECT

One of the characteristics that makes NACWE unique is we are the National Association of <u>Christian</u> Women Entrepreneurs. Respect – it really starts with our relationship with God and then it flows out of us to others. Respect can change lives and attitudes.

SCRIPTURE:

The brave are calling for help. The ambassadors who tried to bring about peace are crying bitterly. The highways are so dangerous that no one travels on them. Treaties are broken and agreements are violated. No one is **respected** any more.
~ **Isaiah 33: 7-8 (Good News Translation)**

"Beware of the teachers of the law. They like to walk around in flowing robes and love to be greeted with **respect** in the marketplaces and have the most important seats in the synagogues and the places of honor at banquets.~ **Luke 20:46 (NIV)**

Show **respect** for all people. Love your brothers and sisters in God's family. **Respect** God, and honor the king.
~ **1 Peter 2:17 (ERV)**

QUOTE: "Respect for ourselves guides our morals, respect for others guides our manners." ~ **Laurence Sterne**

DISCUSSION: When you think of people you respect, what are some of the attributes you see in them? Do you find those same qualities in yourself?

PRAYER: Open for prayer requests.

© 2016 National Association of Christian Women Entrepreneurs * All Rights Reserved * www.nacwe.org

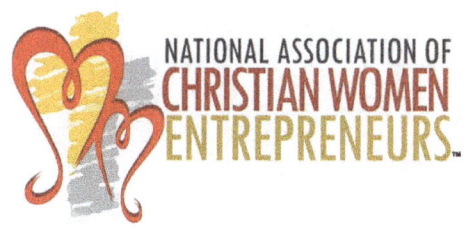

NACWE PRAYER CALL   January 19, 2017
WILLING

One of the characteristics that makes NACWE unique is we are the National Association of <u>Christian</u> Women Entrepreneurs. Are you willing to _____? You fill in the blank. To change, to grow, to be the woman of God He wants you to be first, you need to be willing. Ask Him to help you. He promised He would.

SCRIPTURE:

"And you, my son Solomon, accept the God of your father. Serve him completely and **willingly**, because the Lord knows what is in everyone's mind. He understands everything you think. If you go to him for help, you will get an answer. But if you turn away from him, he will leave you forever." ~ **Isaiah 33: 7-8 (NCV)**

"Restore to me the joy of your salvation and grant me a **willing** spirit, to sustain me." ~ **Psalm 51:12 (NIV)**

"Keep watching and praying that you may not enter into temptation; the spirit is willing, but the flesh is weak."~ **Matthew 26:41 (NASB)**

QUOTE: "Decide what you want, decide what you are willing to exchange for it. Establish your priorities and go to work." ~ **H.L. Hunt**

DISCUSSION: This month we're talking about mindset. What are you willing to do differently in your business this year? If we do the same thing, we will likely get the same results. Are you willing to change?

PRAYER: Open for prayer requests.

© 2016 National Association of Christian Women Entrepreneurs * All Rights Reserved * www.nacwe.org

NACWE PRAYER CALL   January 26, 2017
ENDURANCE

One of the characteristics that makes NACWE unique is we are the National Association of <u>Christian</u> Women Entrepreneurs. You are a woman of great faith ~ a Christian women entrepreneur. Life and being an entrepreneur is a character developer. Through Christ's enduring love and the enduring inheritance, purchased for us, we are called to develop endurance---not just in the times of hardship and suffering but in the little, every day minutia challenges. He has provided the way.

SCRIPTURE:

James 5:10-11 Amplified Bible (AMP)
¹⁰ As an example, brothers and sisters, of suffering and patience, take the prophets who spoke in the name of the Lord [as His messengers and representatives]. ¹¹ You know we call those blessed [happy, spiritually prosperous, favored by God] who were steadfast and endured [difficult circumstances]. You have heard of the patient endurance of Job and you have seen the Lord's outcome [how He richly blessed Job]. The Lord is full of compassion and is merciful.

1 Thessalonians 1:3 International Standard Version (ISV)
³ In the presence of our God and Father, we constantly remember how your faith is active, your love is hard at work, and your <u>hope in our Lord Jesus the Messiah is enduring.</u>

Colossians 1:9-12 (Msg)

Be assured that from the first day we heard of you, we haven't stopped praying for you, asking God to give you wise minds and spirits attuned to his will, and so acquire a thorough understanding of the ways in which God works. We pray that you'll live well for the Master, making him proud of you as you work hard in his orchard. As you learn more and more how God works, you will learn how to do *your* work. We pray that you'll have the strength to stick it out over the long haul—not the grim strength of gritting your teeth but the glory-strength God gives. It is strength that endures the unendurable and spills over into joy, thanking the Father who makes us strong enough to take part in everything bright and beautiful that he has for us.

QUOTE: "Without patient endurance, even the smallest thing becomes unbearable. A lot depends on our attitude." Dalai Lama

DISCUSSION:
1. What is one lesson you have learned through a season of enduring difficult times?
2. In what ways does endurance come into play in your every day life

PRAYER: Open for prayer requests.

© 2016 National Association of Christian Women Entrepreneurs * All Rights Reserved * www.nacwe.org

NACWE PRAYER CALL   February 2, 2017
RENEW

One of the characteristics that makes NACWE unique is we are the National Association of <u>Christian</u> Women Entrepreneurs. The renewing of our minds and our bodies is our goal so that in all things we might let our light shine for Him. Need some renewing and refreshing as we enter the second month of 2017? Me too.

SCRIPTURE:

"Create in me a clean heart, O God; And **renew** a right spirit within me."
~ **Psalm 51:10 (ASV)**

"Who satisfies your desires with good things so that your youth is **renewed** like the eagle's. ~ **Psalm 103:5 (NIV)**

"That's why we are not discouraged. No, even if outwardly we are wearing out, inwardly we are being **renewed** each and every day." ~ **2 Corinthians 4:16 (ISV)**

QUOTE: "I've discovered that when we take time to renew our minds with God's Word, we learn how to think like God thinks, say what God says, and act like He wants us to act." – **Joyce Meyer**

DISCUSSION: What areas are you seeking renewal in your life in 2017? If our minds are renewed, how does it affect the words that we speak?

PRAYER: Open for prayer requests.

© 2016 National Association of Christian Women Entrepreneurs * All Rights Reserved * www.nacwe.org

NACWE PRAYER CALL   February 9, 2017
CONFIDENCE

One of the characteristics that makes NACWE unique is we are the National Association of <u>Christian</u> Women Entrepreneurs. Our greatest source of confidence is Jesus Christ. Without Him, we can do nothing, but with Him, ALL things are possible. Walk in confidence and see what the Lord will do - for you and with you.

SCRIPTURE:

"With him (king of Assyria and his army) is only the arm of flesh, but with us is the Lord our God to help us and to fight our battles." And the people gained **confidence** from what Hezekiah the king of Judah said…"
~ **2 Chronicles 32:8 (NIV)**

"You are my hope, O Almighty Lord. You have been my **confidence** ever since I was young." ~ **Psalm 71:5 (God's WORD version)**

"In him and through faith in him we may approach God with freedom and **confidence**." ~ **Ephesians 3:12 (NIV)**

QUOTE: "Life is not easy for any of us. But what of that? We must have perseverance and above all confidence in ourselves. We must believe that we are gifted for something and that this thing must be attained." – **Marie Curie, Polish scientist, 1st woman to win the Nobel Prize (first person and only woman to win it twice) (1867-1934)**

DISCUSSION: How do you deal with a lack of confidence in your life? Do you ask for help? Run? Hide? Fake it? Boldly move forward?

PRAYER: Open for prayer requests.

© 2016 National Association of Christian Women Entrepreneurs * All Rights Reserved * www.nacwe.org

NACWE PRAYER CALL   February 16, 2017
DEVOTED

One of the characteristics that makes NACWE unique is we are the National Association of <u>Christian</u> Women Entrepreneurs. "Devoted" is defined as having strong love or loyalty for something or someone. Loyalty to God comes first before anyone or anything. My prayer is that this is what people see in you and in your business.

SCRIPTURE:

"For when Solomon was old, his wives turned his heart away after other gods; and his heart was not completely **devoted** to the Lord his God, as was the heart of his father David." ~ **2 Chronicles 32:8 (NIV)**

"No one can serve two masters. Either you will hate the one and love the other, or you will be **devoted** to the one and despise the other. You cannot serve both God and money."~ **Luke 16:13 (NIV)**

"Live in true **devotion** to one another, loving each other as sisters and brothers. Be first to honor others *by putting them first.*" ~ **Romans 10:12 (VOICE)**

QUOTE: "Whatever I have tried to do in life, I have tried with all my heart to do it well; whatever I have devoted myself to, I have devoted myself completely; in great aims and in small I have always thoroughly been in earnest." – **Charles Dickens**

DISCUSSION: Many of us read devotionals as part of our time with God. This captures our devotion in words, but how do you illustrate being devoted through your actions in your life and your business?

PRAYER: Open for prayer requests.

© 2016 National Association of Christian Women Entrepreneurs * All Rights Reserved * www.nacwe.org

NACWE PRAYER CALL   February 23, 2017
PRAISE

One of the characteristics that makes NACWE unique is we are the National Association of Christian Women Entrepreneurs. You are a woman of great faith ~ a Christian women entrepreneur. In life and business, it is not only important to maintain an attitude of praise through the good and the bad, but also to let our life, actions, and work be a praise.   Praise is a lifestyle and we were made for it. He alone is worthy of the highest praise.

SCRIPTURE:
Deuteronomy 10:21 (NASB)
He is your praise and He is your God, who has done these great and awesome things that your eyes have seen.

Joel 2:25-27 (ESV)
I will restore to you the years that the swarming locust has eaten, the hopper, the destroyer, and the cutter, my great army, which I sent among you. You shall eat in plenty and be satisfied, and praise the name of the Lord your God, who has dealt wondrously with you. And my people shall never again be put to shame. You shall know that I am in the midst of Israel and that I am the Lord your God and there is none else.

Ephesians 1:4-6 & 11-12 (NIV)
For he chose us in him before the creation of the world to be holy and blameless in his sight. In love, he predestined us for adoption to sonship through Jesus Christ in accordance with his pleasure and will—to the praise of his glorious grace, which he has freely given us in the One he loves.
11, 12: In him we were also chosen having been predestined according to the plan of him who works out everything in conformity with the purpose of his will, in order that we, who were the first to put our hope in Christ, might be for the praise of his glory.

QUOTE: "Only in the act of praise and worship can a person learn to believe in the goodness and greatness of God." C.S. Lewis

DISCUSSION:
1. What are some examples of praise in your life and business outside of simply saying that praises to Him?

2. God is my praise when _____. I am a Praise to God when I _____.

PRAYER: Open for prayer requests.

© 2016 National Association of Christian Women Entrepreneurs * All Rights Reserved * www.nacwe.org

NACWE PRAYER CALL   March 2, 2017
JOY

One of the characteristics that makes NACWE unique is we are the National Association of Christian Women Entrepreneurs. Joy is the wellspring of life in us. Joy is Jesus living in us and transforming us from the inside out. There is joy in serving Jesus.

SCRIPTURE:

"Nehemiah said, "Go and enjoy choice food and sweet drinks, and send some to those who have nothing prepared. This day is holy to our Lord. Do not grieve, for the **joy** of the Lord is your strength." ~ **Nehemiah 8:10 (NIV)**

"You make known to me the path of life; in your presence there is fullness of **joy**; at your right hand are pleasures forevermore." ~ **Psalm 16:11 (ESV)**

"The women ran quickly from the tomb. They were very frightened but also filled with great **joy**, and they rushed to give the disciples the angel's message."
~ **Matthew 28:8 (NLT)**

QUOTE: "There are souls in this world which have the gift of finding joy everywhere and of leaving it behind them when they go."
– **Jean Paul, German author, 1763-1825**

DISCUSSION: What brings you great joy in your business? In your personal life?

PRAYER: Open for prayer requests.

© 2016 National Association of Christian Women Entrepreneurs * All Rights Reserved * www.nacwe.org

NACWE PRAYER CALL   March 9, 2017
POWERFUL

One of the characteristics that makes NACWE unique is we are the National Association of <u>Christian</u> Women Entrepreneurs. Our power source is Jesus Christ. We are powerful in Him and through Him and He is powerful in and through us. Let your light shine.

SCRIPTURE:

"You might say to yourself, "I am rich because of my own **power** and strength," but remember the L<small>ORD</small> your God! It is he who gives you the **power** to become rich, keeping the agreement he promised to your ancestors, as it is today.
~**Deuteronomy 8:17-18 (NCV)**

"And David became more and more powerful, because the Lord God of Heaven's Armies was with him." ~ **2 Samuel 5:10 (NLT)**

"Therefore confess your sins to each other and pray for each other so that you may be healed. The prayer of a righteous person is **powerful** and effective.
~ **James 5:16 (NIV)**

QUOTE: "When the whole world is silent, even one voice becomes powerful."
— Malala Yousafzai

DISCUSSION: What areas of your life or business do you feel powerful? In your spiritual walk, how do you tap into God's power in your life?

PRAYER: Open for prayer requests.

© 2016 National Association of Christian Women Entrepreneurs * All Rights Reserved * www.nacwe.org

NACWE PRAYER CALL   March 16, 2017
SURRENDER

One of the characteristics that makes NACWE unique is we are the National Association of <u>Christian</u> Women Entrepreneurs. You are a woman of great faith ~ a Christian women entrepreneur. Whatever is done to achieve success in life and business, for the Christian, requires letting go and relinquishing our own ways and thoughts, and surrendering to the higher ways of God whose plans for us are above what we could ever ask or think.

SCRIPTURE:
Wait and listen, everyone who is thirsty! Come to the waters; and he who has no money, come, buy and eat! Yes, come, buy [priceless, spiritual] wine and milk without money and without price [simply for the **self-surrender** that accepts the blessing]. **Isaiah 55:1   AMP**

Yahweh will preserve him, and keep him alive. He shall be blessed on the earth, and he will not **surrender** him to the will of his enemies. **Ps.41:2 NIV**

Just as no one of you who does not detach himself (surrender) from all that belongs to him can be a disciple of mine. **Luke 14:33 WNT**

QUOTE: "The greatness of a man's power is the measure of his surrender." - William Booth

DISCUSSION:

1. What is one of the lessons you have learned through the process of surrender?
2. How has surrendering impacted your business or life?

PRAYER: Open for prayer requests.

© 2016 National Association of Christian Women Entrepreneurs * All Rights Reserved * www.nacwe.org

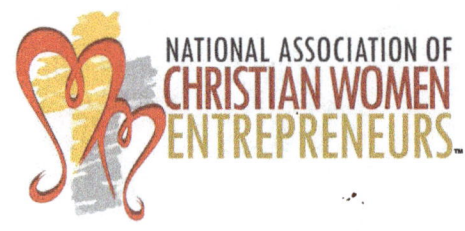

NACWE PRAYER CALL   March 23, 2017
FREEDOM

One of the characteristics that makes NACWE unique is we are the National Association of <u>Christian</u> Women Entrepreneurs. Freedom is not the right to do as you wish at the expense of others. Freedom is a gift that allows you to be all you can be and help others to do the same.

SCRIPTURE:

"I will walk in freedom, for I have devoted myself to your commandments."
~Psalm 119:45 (NLT)

"The Spirit of the Sovereign LORD is on me, because the LORD has anointed me to proclaim good news to the poor. He has sent me to bind up the brokenhearted, to proclaim **freedom** for the captives and release from darkness for the prisoners, to proclaim the year of the LORD's favor and the day of vengeance of our God, to comfort all who mourn." **~Isaiah 61:1-2 (NIV)**

"[*Freedom in Christ*] It is for **freedom** that Christ has set us free. Stand firm, then, and do not let yourselves be burdened again by a yoke of slavery.
~ Galatians 5:1 (NIV)

QUOTE: "A hero is someone who understands the responsibility that comes with his freedom." **~ Bob Dylan**

DISCUSSION: As a believer, how does your freedom in Christ help you unlock the vault of creativity inside of you? What is keeping you from experiencing that freedom that is your birthright as a daughter of the King of kings and the Lord of lords?

PRAYER: Open for prayer requests.

© 2017 National Association of Christian Women Entrepreneurs * All Rights Reserved * www.nacwe.org

NACWE PRAYER CALL   March 30, 2017
HEALING

One of the characteristics that makes NACWE unique is we are the National Association of <u>Christian</u> Women Entrepreneurs. Healing is a gift from God. Healing is needed in every area of our lives – physically, mentally, emotionally and spiritually. God is our Healer. He is the Great Physician.

SCRIPTURE:

"The words of the reckless pierce like swords, but the tongue of the wise brings **healing**." ~**Proverbs 12:18 (NIV)**

""Then my favor will shine on you like the morning sun, and your wounds will be quickly healed. I will always be with you to save you; my presence will protect you on every side." ~**Isaiah 58:8 (GNT)**

"He told her, "Daughter, your faith has made you well. Go in peace and be healed from your illness."~ **Mark 5:34 (ISV)**

QUOTE: "Writing is a way of processing our lives. And it can be a way of healing."
~ **Jan Karon**

DISCUSSION: Question: How has creativity been a healing power in your life? How does your business promote, help or facilitate a pathway to healing for your clients? (not just limited to physical healing)

PRAYER: Open for prayer requests.

© 2017 National Association of Christian Women Entrepreneurs * All Rights Reserved * www.nacwe.org

NACWE PRAYER CALL   April 6, 2017
WORDS

One of the characteristics that makes NACWE unique is we are the National Association of <u>Christian</u> Women Entrepreneurs. Words are powerful. Words have changed the course of history and the course of my life and your life as well. Choose them wisely.

SCRIPTURE:

"Gracious **words** are a honeycomb, sweet to the soul and healing to the bones."
~**Proverbs 16:24 (NIV)**

"Heaven and earth will pass away, but My **words** will not pass away." ~**Matthew 24:35 (NASB)**

"He who was seated on the throne said, "I am making everything new!" Then he said, "Write this down, for these **words** are trustworthy and true."
 ~ **Revelation 21:5 (NIV)**

QUOTE: "In prayer it is better to have a heart without words than words without a heart." ~ **Mahatma Gandhi**

DISCUSSION: Words are the tool of every writer. What is your greatest struggle with words?

PRAYER: Open for prayer requests.

© 2017 National Association of Christian Women Entrepreneurs * All Rights Reserved * www.nacwe.org

NACWE PRAYER CALL   April 13, 2017
THOUGHTS

One of the characteristics that makes NACWE unique is we are the National Association of <u>Christian</u> Women Entrepreneurs. Our thoughts are the seeds that turn into words and actions. What do you think about? How do your thoughts change the course of your life?

SCRIPTURE:

"The wicked people are too proud. They do not look for God; there is no room for God in their **thoughts**." ~**Psalm 10:4 (NCV)**

"For *as* the heavens are higher than the earth, so are My ways higher than your ways And My **thoughts** than your **thoughts**." ~**Isaiah 55:9 (ESV)**

"*We are* destroying sophisticated arguments and every exalted *and* proud thing that sets itself up against the [true] knowledge of God, and *we are* taking every **thought** *and* purpose captive to the obedience of Christ." ~ **2 Corinthians 10:5 (AMP)**

QUOTE: "The worst bullies you will ever encounter in your life are your own thoughts." ~ **Bryant H. McGill**

DISCUSSION: Take a moment to focus on either your business or your personal life and consider how your thoughts are opening doors for you or destroying opportunities. Please share a victory moment with us.

PRAYER: Open for prayer requests.

© 2017 National Association of Christian Women Entrepreneurs * All Rights Reserved * www.nacwe.org

NACWE PRAYER CALL   April 20, 2017
ACTIONS

One of the characteristics that makes NACWE unique is we are the National Association of <u>Christian</u> Women Entrepreneurs. So far this month we have talked about "words" and "thoughts" but that is not enough. We must take action. Our actions speak louder than our words.

SCRIPTURE:

"They will be My people, and I will be their God; I will give them singleness of heart and **action**, so that they will always fear me and that all will then go well for them and for their children after them." ~**Jeremiah 32:38-39 (NIV)**

"You see that his (Abraham's) faith and his **actions** were working together, and his faith was made complete by what he did." ~**James 2:22 (NIV)**

"Little children, we must stop expressing love merely by our words and manner of speech; we must love also in **action** and in truth." ~ **1 John 3:18 (ISV)**

QUOTE: "If your **actions** inspire others to dream more, learn more, do more and become more, you are a leader." ~ **John Quincy Adams**

DISCUSSION: We have often heard the saying, "Actions speak louder than words." Are there areas of your life/business where you are having difficulty translating your words into actions? If so, can you identify the obstacle?

PRAYER: Open for prayer requests.

© 2017 National Association of Christian Women Entrepreneurs * All Rights Reserved * www.nacwe.org

NACWE PRAYER CALL   April 27, 2017
ENCOURAGE

One of the characteristics that makes NACWE unique is we are the National Association of Christian Women Entrepreneurs. You are a woman of great faith ~ a Christian women entrepreneur. No one does this journey or life by themselves. As a Christian woman entrepreneur, you were meant to encourage and be encouraged. We need each other. Our words and our voices were made to impact each other.

SCRIPTURE:
When he arrived, and saw the grace of God (that was bestowed on them), he rejoiced and began to encourage them all with an unwavering heart to stay true and devoted to the Lord. For Barnabas was a good man (privately and publicly-his Godly character benefited himself and others) and he was full of the Holy Spirit and full of faith in Jesus the Messiah, through home believers have everlasting life. **Acts 11:23-24 AMP**

So when they were sent off, they went down to Antioch: and after assembling the congregation, they delivered the letter.   And when they had read it, the people rejoiced greatly at the encouragement and comfort it brought them. Judas and Silas, who were themselves prophets (divinely inspired spokesmen), encouraged and strengthened the believers with many words.   **Acts 15:30-32 AMP**

Now may the God of peace (the source of serenity and spiritual well-being) who brought up from the dead our Lord Jesus, the great Shepherd of the sheep, through the blood that sealed and ratified the eternal covenant, equip you with every good thing to carry out His will and strengthen you (making you complete and perfect as you ought to be), accomplishing in us that which is pleasing in His sight, through Jesus Christ, to whom be the glory forever and ever. Amen. I call on you brothers and sisters, listen patiently to this message of exhortation and encouragement, for I have written you briefly.   **Hebrews 13: 20-22 AMP**

QUOTE: "A word of encouragement during failure is worth more than an hour of praise after success." Unknown

DISCUSSION:

1. What is one of the most encouraging words you ever read or had spoken to you?
2. What steps could you take to be a better encourager?

PRAYER: Open for prayer requests.

© 2016 National Association of Christian Women Entrepreneurs * All Rights Reserved * www.nacwe.org

NACWE PRAYER CALL   May 4, 2017
HONOR

One of the characteristics that makes NACWE unique is we are the National Association of Christian Women Entrepreneurs. Honor means to regard with great respect. Our discussion today is a good reminder to honor our clients, regard them with great respect. It is in honoring others that we will be honored by God.

SCRIPTURE:

"**Honor** your father and your mother, as the Lord your God has commanded you, so that you may live long and that it may go well with you in the land the Lord your God is giving you." ~**Deuteronomy 5:16 (NIV)**

"If any of you wants to serve me, then follow me. Then you'll be where I am, ready to serve at a moment's notice. The Father will **honor** and reward anyone who serves me." ~**John 12:26 (MSG)**

"You are worthy, O Lord, To receive glory and **honor** and power; For You created all things, And by Your will they exist and were created."~ **Revelation 4:11 (NKJV)**

QUOTE: "It is not the honor that you take with you, but the heritage you leave behind. ~ **Branch Richey**

DISCUSSION: Last weekend at the NACWE conference we talked about legacy, our stories. What is the heritage you want to leave behind?

PRAYER: Open for prayer requests.

© 2017 National Association of Christian Women Entrepreneurs * All Rights Reserved * www.nacwe.org

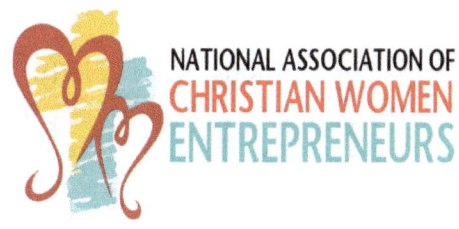

NACWE PRAYER CALL   May 11, 2017
CELEBRATE

One of the characteristics that makes NACWE unique is we are the National Association of <u>Christian</u> Women Entrepreneurs. Celebration – a time to stop and remember and rejoice and give thanks. This week we are celebrating NACWE's 7th birthday, but we should rejoice every day for what the Lord has done!

SCRIPTURE:

"So all the people went to Gilgal and made Saul king in the presence of the Lord. There they sacrificed fellowship offerings before the Lord, and Saul and all the Israelites held a great **celebration**." ~ **1 Samuel 11:15 (NIV)**

"Then David said to Michal, "The Lord chose me, not your father or anyone from his family. The Lord chose me to be leader of his people, the Israelites. So I will continue dancing and **celebrating** in front of the Lord." ~ **2 Samuel 6:21 (ERV)**

"But it was fitting to **celebrate** and rejoice, for this brother of yours was [as good as] dead and *has begun* to live. He was lost and has been found."~ **Luke 15:32 (AMP)**

QUOTE: "Celebrate your successes. Find some humor in your failures."
~ Sam Walton

DISCUSSION: Have you learned to celebrate your successes and the lessons learned from what some people might call "failures"? What have you learned about yourself?

PRAYER: Open for prayer requests.

© 2017 National Association of Christian Women Entrepreneurs * All Rights Reserved * www.nacwe.org

NACWE PRAYER CALL   May 18, 2017
PRESENCE

One of the characteristics that makes NACWE unique is we are the National Association of <u>Christian</u> Women Entrepreneurs. Presence is defined as "being present or a noteworthy quality of poise or effectiveness." When the presence of the Lord is with us, we are powerful and effective. Press into Him and His presence will transform you, your business, your life, and your clients.

SCRIPTURE:

"You make known to me the path of life; in your **presence** there is fullness of joy; at your right hand are pleasures forevermore." ~ **Psalm 16:11 (ESV)**

"Then the woman, seeing that she could not go unnoticed, came trembling and fell at his feet. In the **presence** of all the people, she told why she had touched him and how she had been instantly healed."~ **Luke 8:47 (NIV)**

"Now unto him that is able to keep you from falling, and to present you faultless before the **presence** of his glory with exceeding joy, to the only wise God our Savior, be glory and majesty, dominion and power, both now and ever. Amen." (Doxology)
~ **Jude 24-25 (KJV)**

QUOTE: "Presence is more than just being there." ~ **Malcom Forbes**

DISCUSSION: When thinking about your business, has your "presence" changed as your business has grown? Describe how you are "different" than on the day you first opened your business.

PRAYER: Open for prayer requests.

NACWE PRAYER CALL   May 25, 2017
SERVE

One of the characteristics that makes NACWE unique is we are the National Association of <u>Christian</u> Women Entrepreneurs. Jesus came to serve and not be served. Where is God calling you to serve today and in the days to come?

SCRIPTURE:

"But if serving the Lord seems undesirable to you, then choose for yourselves this day whom you will **serve**, whether the gods your ancestors **serve**d beyond the Euphrates, or the gods of the Amorites, in whose land you are living. But as for me and my household, we will **serve** the Lord." ~ **Joshua 24:15 (NIV)**

"…just as the Son of Man did not come to be **served**, but to **serve**, and to give his life as a ransom for many." ~ **Matthew 20:28 (NIV)**

"Do your work with enthusiasm. Work as if you were **serving** the Lord, not as if you were serving only men and women." ~ **Ephesians 6:7 (NCV)**

QUOTE: "Memorial Day isn't just about honoring veterans, its honoring those who lost their lives. Veterans had the fortune of coming home. For us, that's a reminder of when we come home we still have a <u>responsibility to serve</u>. It's a continuation of service that honors our country and those who fell defending it." ~ **Pete Hegseth, U.S. veteran**

DISCUSSION: We are called to serve our clients with the same enthusiasm as we serve the Lord. What are the areas you struggle with as you serve your clients?

PRAYER: Open for prayer requests.

© 2017 National Association of Christian Women Entrepreneurs * All Rights Reserved * www.nacwe.org

NACWE PRAYER CALL   June 1, 2017
PROTECT

One of the characteristics that makes NACWE unique is we are the National Association of <u>Christian</u> Women Entrepreneurs. The Lord protects His children like a hen protects her chicks. He is your shield and your defender. Who are we called to protect as His ambassadors here on earth?

SCRIPTURE:

"Because he loves me," says the Lord, "I will rescue him; I will **protect** him, for he acknowledges my name." ~ **Psalm 91:14 (NIV)**

"For He guards the course of the just and **protects** the way of His faithful ones."
~ **Proverbs 2:8 (NIV)**

"But the Lord is faithful, and He will strengthen you [setting you on a firm foundation] and will **protect** *and* guard you from the evil *one*." ~ **2 Thessalonians 3:3 (AMP)**

QUOTE: "God is never on the sidelines of His children's lives. He goes before them. He leads them, guides them, protects and saves them." ~ **Monica Johnson,** American Writer

DISCUSSION: How are we, as entrepreneurs, called to protect the legacy of women business owners, past, present, and future?

PRAYER: Open for prayer requests.

© 2017 National Association of Christian Women Entrepreneurs * All Rights Reserved * www.nacwe.org

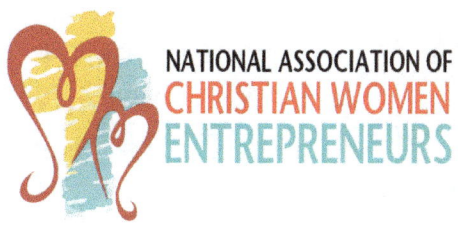

NACWE PRAYER CALL   June 8, 2017
ANXIETY (ANXIOUS)

One of the characteristics that makes NACWE unique is we are the National Association of <u>Christian</u> Women Entrepreneurs. The Lord tells us not to worry, not to be anxious about anything, but it can be challenging some days. We are to exchange our anxious thoughts for His peace.

SCRIPTURE:

"Search me, O God, and know my heart; Try me and know my anxious thoughts."
~ **Psalm 139:23**

"Do not be **anxious** *or* worried about anything, but in everything [every circumstance and situation] by prayer and petition with thanksgiving, continue to make your [specific] requests known to God." ~ **Philippians 4:6 (AMP)**

"Cast all your **anxiety** on him because he cares for you." ~ **1 Peter 5:7 (NIV)**

QUOTE: "Anxiety does not empty tomorrow of its sorrows, but only empties today of its strength." ~ **Charles Spurgeon**

DISCUSSION: Why are we talking about anxiety today and being anxious? As business owners, we have moments of anxiety/worry about our life, our family, and our businesses. What is one positive way that has helped you deal with your concerns?

PRAYER: Open for prayer requests.

© 2017 National Association of Christian Women Entrepreneurs * All Rights Reserved * www.nacwe.org

NACWE PRAYER CALL   June 15, 2017
TIME

One of the characteristics that makes NACWE unique is we are the National Association of <u>Christian</u> Women Entrepreneurs. Time is a gift. We can squander it or use it for God's glory. Is "redeeming" time a challenge for you?

SCRIPTURE:

"He has made everything beautiful in its **time**. He has also set eternity in the human heart; yet no one can fathom what God has done from beginning to end."
~ **Ecclesiastes 3:11 (NIV)**

"But do not overlook this one fact, beloved, that with the Lord one day is as a thousand years, and a thousand years as one day." ~ **2 Peter 3:8 (ESV)**

"But when the fullness of **time** had come, God sent forth his Son, born of woman, born under the law, to redeem those who were under the law, so that we might receive adoption as sons." ~ **Galatians 4:4-5 (ESV)**

QUOTE: "The **time** to relax is when you don't have time for it." ~ **Sydney J. Harris**

DISCUSSION: Is time your friend or your enemy? And any tips you'd like to share with your sisters about time challenges – what works and what doesn't.

PRAYER: Open for prayer requests.

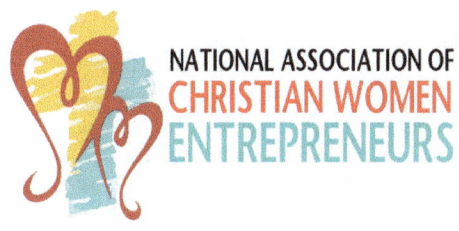

NACWE PRAYER CALL   June 22, 2017
COMFORT

One of the characteristics that makes NACWE unique is we are the National Association of <u>Christian</u> Women Entrepreneurs. He is the God of all comfort and He calls us to comfort one another even as He has comforted us.

SCRIPTURE:

"Even though I walk through the darkest valley, I will fear no evil, for you are with me; your rod and your staff, they **comfort** me."~ **Psalm 23:4 (NIV)**

"This is my **comfort** in my affliction, That <u>Your word</u> has revived me *and* given me life." ~ **Psalm 119:50 (AMP)**

"Who **comfort**s us in all our troubles, so that we can **comfort** those in any trouble with the **comfort** we ourselves receive from God."~ **2 Corinthians 1:4 (NIV)**

QUOTE: *"Comfort and prosperity have never enriched the world as much as adversity has."* ~ **Billy Graham**

DISCUSSION: As business owners, there are times we are called to be the 'comforters' and other times we are called to be 'comforted.' Which is easier for you?

PRAYER: Open for prayer requests.

© 2017 National Association of Christian Women Entrepreneurs * All Rights Reserved * www.nacwe.org

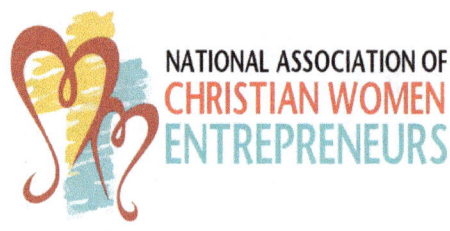

NACWE PRAYER CALL   June 29, 2017
REJOICE!

One of the characteristics that makes NACWE unique is we are the National Association of <u>Christian</u> Women Entrepreneurs. The word "rejoice" means to feel joy or great delight. Just the sound of the word can make you happy. Do you let that joy permeate every circumstance in your life – good or not so good? Rejoice, and again, I say, REJOICE!

SCRIPTURE:

"Shout for joy, you heavens; **rejoice**, you earth; burst into song, you mountains! For the Lord comforts his people and will have compassion on his afflicted ones."
~ Isaiah 49:13 (NIV)

"Do not gaze *and* gloat [in triumph] over your brother's day, the day when his misfortune came. Do not rejoice over the sons of Judah in the day of their destruction; Do not speak arrogantly [jeering and maliciously mocking] in the day of their distress."
~ Obadiah 1:12 (AMP)

"And when she finds it, she calls her friends and neighbors together and says, '**Rejoice with me; I have found my lost coin.**'"**~ Luke 15:9 (NIV)**

QUOTE: "Satan wants us to constantly focus on everything that is wrong with us and look at how far we still have to go. But God desires for us to **rejoice** in how far we have already come." **~ Joyce Meyer**

DISCUSSION: Please share with us an opportunity you have chosen to rejoice this last week – in your business or your personal life.

PRAYER: Open for prayer requests.

© 2017 National Association of Christian Women Entrepreneurs * All Rights Reserved * www.nacwe.org

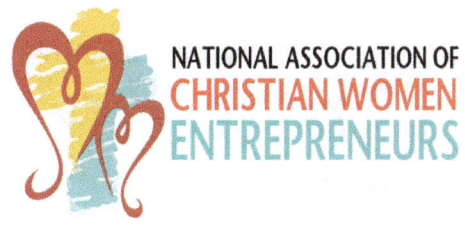

NACWE PRAYER CALL   July 6, 2017
KINDNESS

One of the characteristics that makes NACWE unique is we are the National Association of <u>Christian</u> Women Entrepreneurs. Social media is a place where many emotions are displayed. Kindness is a virtue that is welcome there. Spread a little kindness wherever you go.

SCRIPTURE:

"Then Naomi said to her two daughters-in-law, "Go back, each of you, to your mother's home. May the Lord show you **kindness**, as you have shown **kindness** to your dead husbands and to me." ~ **Ruth 1:8 (NIV)**

"But Hezekiah's heart was proud and he did not respond to the **kindness** shown him; therefore the Lord's wrath was on him and on Judah and Jerusalem."
~ **2 Chronicles 32:25 (NIV)**

"I will tell of the **kindnesses** of the Lord, the deeds for which he is to be praised, according to all the Lord has done for us— yes, the many good things he has done for Israel, according to his compassion and many **kindnesses**." ~ **Isaiah 63:7 (NIV)**

QUOTE: "Kindness is the language which the deaf can hear and the blind can see."
~ **Mark Twain**

DISCUSSION: How has kindness impacted your personal life and/or your business?

PRAYER: Open for prayer requests.

© 2017 National Association of Christian Women Entrepreneurs * All Rights Reserved * www.nacwe.org

NACWE PRAYER CALL   July 13, 2017
HUMILITY

One of the characteristics that makes NACWE unique is we are the National Association of <u>Christian</u> Women Entrepreneurs. Humility is often spoken of as the hallmark of a good leader. The word is defined as "freedom from pride or arrogance." Jesus is the ultimate example of a man of great humility. Let us follow in His steps.

SCRIPTURE:

"**Humility** and reverence for the Lord will make you both wise and honored."
~ **Proverbs 15:33 (TLB)**

"Therefore, as God's chosen people, holy and dearly loved, clothe yourselves with compassion, kindness, **humility**, gentleness and patience."
~ **Colossians 3:12 (NIV)**

"Likewise, you younger men [of lesser rank and experience], be subject to your elders [seek their counsel]; and all of you, clothe yourselves with **humility** toward one another [tie on the servant's apron], for God is opposed to the proud [the disdainful, the presumptuous, and He defeats them], but He gives grace to the humble. Therefore humble yourselves under the mighty hand of God [set aside self-righteous pride], so that He may exalt you [to a place of honor in His service] at the appropriate time."
~ **1 Peter 5:5-6 (AMP)**

QUOTE: "The principles of living greatly include the capacity to face trouble with courage, disappointment with cheerfulness, and trial with humility."
~ **Thomas S. Monson**

DISCUSSION: When you think about humility, are you humble because of what you do or the things you don't do? How does humility play a role in the business world?

PRAYER: Open for prayer requests.

© 2017 National Association of Christian Women Entrepreneurs * All Rights Reserved * www.nacwe.org

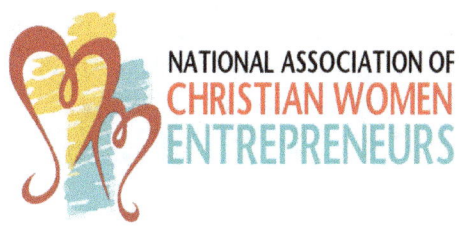

Conference Call Phone #: 302.202.1119 PIN: 173198

NACWE PRAYER CALL   July 20, 2017
SUPPORT

One of the characteristics that makes NACWE unique is we are the National Association of <u>Christian</u> Women Entrepreneurs. We all need support. Life is not meant to be lived alone; businesses cannot thrive with the "Lone Ranger" mentality. The Lord is our 24/7 support system but sometimes we need help "with skin on". We are here to support each other; NACWE is here to support you.

SCRIPTURE:

"When I said, "My foot is slipping," your unfailing love, Lord, **supported** me."
~ **Psalm 94:18 (NIV)**

"Now these are the chiefs of David's mighty men, who gave him strong **support** in his kingdom, together with all Israel, to make him king, according to the word of the Lord concerning Israel." ~ **1 Chronicles 11:10 (ESV)**

"Your words have **supported** those who stumbled, and you have strengthened the knees that gave way." ~ **Job 4:4 (NET)**

QUOTE: "You can do anything as long as you have the passion, the drive, the focus, and the support." ~ **Sabrina Bryan**

DISCUSSION: Do you have a support system in your life and business? How has NACWE filled that role as "life support" for you?

PRAYER: Open for prayer requests.

© 2017 National Association of Christian Women Entrepreneurs * All Rights Reserved * www.nacwe.org

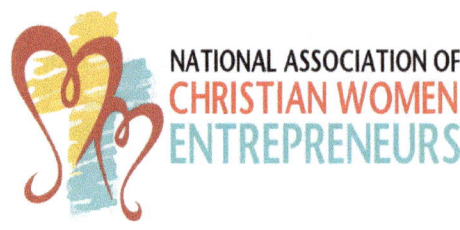

Conference Call Phone #: 302.202.1119 PIN: 173198

NACWE PRAYER CALL   July 27, 2017
TREASURE

One of the characteristics that makes NACWE unique is we are the National Association of <u>Christian</u> Women Entrepreneurs. You are treasured by your heavenly Father. Do you believe it? It's time to receive it. There is hidden treasure buried in you and me. The world needs what we have, it's time to get started.

SCRIPTURE:

"They will be Mine," says the Lord of hosts, "on that day when I publicly recognize them *and* openly declare them to be My own possession [that is, **My very special treasure**]. And I will have compassion on them *and* spare them as a man spares his own son who serves him." ~ **Malachi 3:17 (AMP)**

"Don't hoard **treasure** down here where it gets eaten by moths and corroded by rust or—worse!—stolen by burglars. Stockpile **treasure** in heaven, where it's safe from moth and rust and burglars. It's obvious, isn't it? The place where your **treasure** is, is the place you will most want to be, and end up being." ~ **Matthew 6:19 (MSG)**

"But we have this **treasure** in jars of clay to show that this all-surpassing power is from God and not from us." ~ **2 Corinthians 4:7 (NIV)**

QUOTE: "The fears you run away from run toward you. The fears you don't own will own you. But behind every fear wall lives a precious treasure." ~ **Robin S. Sharma**

DISCUSSION: Most of us still have hidden treasure buried deep inside of us. What "tools" do you use to mine that treasure in both yourself and your clients?

PRAYER: Open for prayer requests.

© 2017 National Association of Christian Women Entrepreneurs * All Rights Reserved * www.nacwe.org

Conference Call Phone #: 302.202.1119 PIN: 173198

NACWE PRAYER CALL   August 3, 2017
APPEARANCE

One of the characteristics that makes NACWE unique is we are the National Association of <u>Christian</u> Women Entrepreneurs. Our appearance in person or online speaks volumes about who we are. Does what you do and say and write and speak let people know you are a Christian? Is that important to you? to God?

SCRIPTURE:

"But the Lord said to Samuel, "Do not consider his **appearance** or his height, for I have rejected him. The Lord does not look at the things people look at. People look at the outward **appearance**, but the Lord looks at the heart."~ **1 Samuel 16:7 (NIV)**

"He grew up like a small plant before the Lord, like a root growing in a dry land. He had no special beauty or form to make us notice him; there was nothing in his **appearance** to make us desire him." ~ **Isaiah 53:2 (NCV)**

"While he was praying, the **appearance** of his face changed, and his clothes turned dazzling white." ~ **Luke 9:29 (NIV)**

QUOTE: "I don't understand why the press is so interested in speculating about my appearance, anyway. What does my face have to do with my music or my dancing?"
~ **Michael Jackson**

DISCUSSION: When we think about branding, not only a business owner but as a consumer, what does the appearance of a product, or a person, have to do with the quality of the product/service? Do you still judge a book by its cover?

PRAYER: Open for prayer requests.

© 2017 National Association of Christian Women Entrepreneurs * All Rights Reserved * www.nacwe.org

Conference Call Phone #: 302.202.1119 PIN: 173198

NACWE PRAYER CALL   August 10, 2017
DECLARE

One of the characteristics that makes NACWE unique is we are the National Association of <u>Christian</u> Women Entrepreneurs. One of the definitions of declare in the dictionary is "to make known emphatically." In the times in which we live, I believe as Christian women, we need to speak the truth <u>emphatically</u> to ourselves and others. God's word needs to permeate our minds as we push back the darkness and lies of the world. Declare the Word of the Lord!

SCRIPTURE:

"The heavens **declare** the glory of God, and the sky above proclaims his handiwork."
~ **Psalm 19:1 (ESV)**

"And you, my sheep, the sheep of my pasture, are my people, and I am your God, **declares** the sovereign LORD." ~ **Ezekiel 34:31 (NEV)**

"Pray also for me, that whenever I speak, words may be given me so that I will fearlessly make known the mystery of the gospel, for which I am an ambassador in chains. Pray that I may **declare** it fearlessly, as I should."
~ **Ephesians 6: 19-20 (NIV)**

QUOTE: "The opportunity to declare a truth may come when we least expect it. Let us be prepared." ~ **Thomas S. Monson**

© 2017 National Association of Christian Women Entrepreneurs * All Rights Reserved * www.nacwe.org

Conference Call Phone #: 302.202.1119 PIN: 173198

NACWE PRAYER CALL   August 17, 2017
COMPASSION

One of the characteristics that makes NACWE unique is we are the National Association of <u>Christian</u> Women Entrepreneurs. The Lord's compassion never fails, but does ours? The marketplace can be devoid of compassion, but as Christian woman entrepreneurs we are called to be kind and compassionate and let our light shine.

SCRIPTURE:

"You, in Your great **compassion**, Did not forsake them in the wilderness; The pillar of cloud did not leave them by day, To guide them on their way, Nor the pillar of fire by night, to light for them the way in which they were to go."~ **Nehemiah 9:19 (NASB)**

"This is what the LORD Almighty said: 'Administer true justice; show mercy and **compassion** to one another.'" ~ **Zechariah 7:9 (NIV)**

"When he saw the crowds, he felt sorry [had **compassion**] for them because they were hurting [distressed; confused; harassed] and helpless [discouraged; dejected], like sheep without a shepherd." ~ **Matthew 9:36 (EXB)**

QUOTE: "True compassion means not only feeling another's pain but also being moved to help relieve it." ~ **Daniel Goleman**

DISCUSSION: How is compassion a part of your life – both in your business/ministry and your personal life? Do you think society ever views compassion as a weakness?

PRAYER: Open for prayer requests.

© 2017 National Association of Christian Women Entrepreneurs * All Rights Reserved * www.nacwe.org

Conference Call Phone #: 302.202.1119 PIN: 173198

NACWE PRAYER CALL   August 24, 2017
MOUNTAINS

One of the characteristics that makes NACWE unique is we are the National Association of <u>Christian</u> Women Entrepreneurs. Snow-capped mountains may be a beautiful sight but climbing life's mountains can wear you out. Are you grateful that God is the mountain mover? There is nothing too hard for Him.

SCRIPTURE:

"Your righteousness is like the highest mountains, your justice like the great deep. You, LORD, preserve both people and animals." ~ **Psalm 36:6 (NIV)**

"I will go before you and level the mountains [to make the crooked places straight]; I will break in pieces the doors of bronze and cut asunder the bars of iron."
~ **Isaiah 45:2 (AMPC)**

"And after he had dismissed the crowds, he went up on the mountain by himself to pray. When evening came, he was there alone." ~ **Matthew 14:23 (ESV)**

QUOTE: "I'm one of those people who always needs a mountain to climb. When I get up a mountain as far as I think I'm going to get, I try to find another mountain."
~ **Polly Bergen**

DISCUSSION: Looking at the quote, do you believe that's especially true for entrepreneurs? Is this true in your own life? Reflect on a mountain you are facing right now, what kind of help do you need to overcome it?

PRAYER: Open for prayer requests.

© 2017 National Association of Christian Women Entrepreneurs * All Rights Reserved * www.nacwe.org

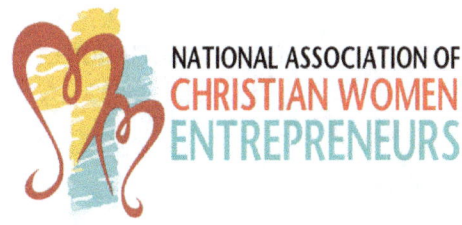

Conference Call Phone #: 302.202.1119 PIN: 173198

NACWE PRAYER CALL   August 31, 2017
KNOWLEDGE

One of the characteristics that makes NACWE unique is we are the National Association of <u>Christian</u> Women Entrepreneurs. We may have a lot of "book knowledge" but how does it change our lives? Jesus calls us into a deeper more intimate relationship with Him every day. Think about how you will take action today.

SCRIPTURE:

"Give me wisdom and **knowledge**, that I may lead this people, for who is able to govern this great people of yours?" ~ **2 Chronicles 1:10 (NIV)**

"Whoever loves discipline loves **knowledge**, but he who hates reproof is stupid (foolish)." ~ **Proverbs 12:1 (ESV)**

"For His divine power has bestowed on us [absolutely] everything necessary for [a dynamic spiritual] life and godliness, through true *and* personal **knowledge** of Him who called us by His own glory and excellence." ~ **2 Peter 1:3 (AMP)**

QUOTE: "The goal of education is the advancement of knowledge and the dissemination of truth." ~ **John F. Kennedy**

DISCUSSION: In your business how do you weave what you have learned (knowledge) with Jesus' call to be His hands and feet? Is that a challenge for you?

PRAYER: Open for prayer requests.

© 2017 National Association of Christian Women Entrepreneurs * All Rights Reserved * www.nacwe.org

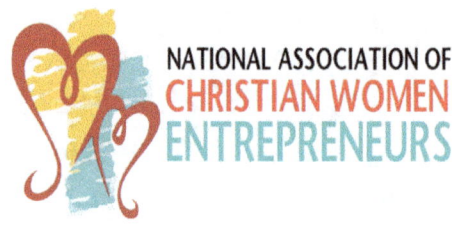

NATIONAL ASSOCIATION OF CHRISTIAN WOMEN ENTREPRENEURS

Conference Call Phone #: 302.202.1119 PIN: 173198

NACWE PRAYER CALL   September 7, 2017
BLESSING

One of the characteristics that makes NACWE unique is we are the National Association of <u>Christian</u> Women Entrepreneurs. This month NACWE's focus is on strategic planning. Planning creates targeted opportunities to be a blessing to others. As we walk forward, we become focused on doing the work God has for us to do. We are blessed to be a blessing.

SCRIPTURE:

"When Joseph was put in charge of the house and everything Potiphar owned, the LORD blessed the people in Potiphar's house because of Joseph. And the LORD blessed everything that belonged to Potiphar, both in the house and in the field."
~ Genesis 39:5 (NCV)

"You will eat the fruit of your labor; blessings and prosperity will be yours."
~ Psalm 128:2 (NIV)

"And never return evil for evil or insult for insult [avoid scolding, berating, and any kind of abuse], but on the contrary, give a blessing [pray for one another's well-being, contentment, and protection]; for you have been called for this very purpose, that you might inherit a blessing [from God that brings well-being, happiness, and protection]."
~ 1 Peter 3:9 (AMP)

QUOTE: "Each time we cooperate with God, we take one more giant step forward. Because when God asks us to change, it means that He always has something better to give us - more freedom, greater joy, and greater blessings."~ **Joyce Meyer**

DISCUSSION: How is God using you in your business/ministry to be a blessing to others?

PRAYER: Open for prayer requests.

© 2017 National Association of Christian Women Entrepreneurs * All Rights Reserved * www.nacwe.org

Conference Call Phone #: 302.202.1119 PIN: 173198

NACWE PRAYER CALL   September 14, 2017
ORDER

One of the characteristics that makes NACWE unique is we are the National Association of <u>Christian</u> Women Entrepreneurs. This month NACWE's focus is on strategic planning. When God created the earth, He brought order out of the chaos. He wants us to do the same in our lives. He is a God of order.

SCRIPTURE:

"You shall be in charge of my palace, and all my people are to submit to your orders. Only with respect to the throne will I be greater than you." ~ **Genesis 41:40 (NIV)**

"But all things should be done decently and in order."~ **1 Corinthians 14:40 (ESV)**

"He will wipe every tear from their eyes. There will be no more death or mourning or crying or pain, for the old order of things has passed away." ~ **Revelation 21:4 (NIV)**

QUOTE: "The result showed the wisdom of your orders." ~ John Bigelow, Lawyer

DISCUSSION: How do you keep your life/business in order? Share a routine or tool or practice that helps you do so.

PRAYER: Open for prayer requests.

© 2017 National Association of Christian Women Entrepreneurs * All Rights Reserved * www.nacwe.org

Conference Call Phone #: 302.202.1119 PIN: 173198

NACWE PRAYER CALL   September 21, 2017
DEPEND

One of the characteristics that makes NACWE unique is we are the National Association of <u>Christian</u> Women Entrepreneurs. We can always depend on God, in the calm or in the storm. It's not a sign of weakness to lean on your heavenly Father. In fact, it's a sign of strength.

SCRIPTURE:

"But perhaps you will say to me, 'We are trusting in the LORD our God!' But isn't he the one who was insulted by Hezekiah? Didn't Hezekiah tear down his shrines and altars and make everyone in Judah and Jerusalem worship only at the altar here in Jerusalem?"~ **2 Kings 18:22 (NLT)**

"My salvation and my honor depend on God; he is my mighty rock, my refuge."
~ **Psalm 62:7 (NIV)**

"If it is possible, as far as it depends on you, live at peace with everyone."
~ **Romans 12:18 (NIV)**

QUOTE: "Happiness is inward, and not outward; and so, it does not depend on what we have, but on what we are." ~ Henry Van Dyke

DISCUSSION: Are you comfortable depending on God or does your independent entrepreneurial spirit desire to walk alone?

PRAYER: Open for prayer requests.

© 2017 National Association of Christian Women Entrepreneurs * All Rights Reserved * www.nacwe.org

Conference Call Phone #: 302.202.1119 PIN: 173198

NACWE PRAYER CALL   September 28, 2017
GLORY

One of the characteristics that makes NACWE unique is we are the National Association of <u>Christian</u> Women Entrepreneurs. In the world, people often seek their own glory. As believers, our desire is to see God honored and glorified. To God be the glory!

SCRIPTURE:

"Who among the gods is like you, LORD? Who is like you— majestic in holiness, awesome in glory, working wonders?" **Exodus 15:11 (NIV)**

"The heavens declare the glory of God; the skies proclaim the work of his hands." **Psalm 19:1 (NIV)**

"So whether you eat or drink or whatever you do, do it all for the glory of God." **1 Corinthians 10:31 (NIV)**

QUOTE: "I give all the glory to God. It's kind of a win-win situation. The glory goes up to Him and the blessings fall down on me." Gabby Douglas, Olympic Gymnast

DISCUSSION: Is there a mindset shift that happens when we dedicate our work to God's glory and not our own? What happens when our aim is for His glory?

PRAYER: Open for prayer requests.

© 2017 National Association of Christian Women Entrepreneurs * All Rights Reserved * www.nacwe.org

Conference Call Phone #: 302.202.1119 PIN: 173198

NACWE PRAYER CALL   October 5, 2017
BELIEVE

One of the characteristics that makes NACWE unique is we are the National Association of <u>Christian</u> Women Entrepreneurs. Only believe… it sounds so simple but it can be one of our greatest struggles as believers and human beings. The Bible is filled with miracles when people believed in Jesus. It's no different today.

SCRIPTURE:

"[*Signs for Moses*] Moses answered, "What if they do not believe me or listen to me and say, 'The LORD did not appear to you'?" **Exodus 14:1 (NIV)**

"I have spoken to you of earthly things and you do not believe; how then will you believe if I speak of heavenly things?" **John 3:12 (NIV)**

"But when you ask, you must believe and not doubt, because the one who doubts is like a wave of the sea, blown and tossed by the wind." **James 1:6 (NIV)**

QUOTE: "The future belongs to those who believe in the beauty of their dreams."
~Eleanor Roosevelt

DISCUSSION: Is there something you struggle believing about yourself in your business or in your personal life? How has that held you back from succeeding?

PRAYER: Open for prayer requests.

© 2017 National Association of Christian Women Entrepreneurs * All Rights Reserved * www.nacwe.org

Conference Call Phone #: 302.202.1119 PIN: 173198

NACWE PRAYER CALL   October 12, 2017
MONEY

One of the characteristics that makes NACWE unique is we are the National Association of <u>Christian</u> Women Entrepreneurs. We are talking about money and finances this month in NACWE. Money is a necessity in the world in which we live. Our pursuit of money, or its pursuit of us, is an indication of whom or what is sitting on the throne of our life – God or money. We can't serve both masters.

SCRIPTURE:

"And when the money was all spent in the land of Egypt and in the land of Canaan, all the Egyptians came to Joseph and said, "Give us food. Why should we die before your eyes? For our money is gone." **Genesis 47:15 (ESV)**

"No one can serve two masters. Either you will hate the one and love the other, or you will be devoted to the one and despise the other. You cannot serve both God and money." **Matthew 21:12 (NIV)**

"For the love of money [that is, the greedy desire for it and the willingness to gain it unethically] is a root of all sorts of evil, and some by longing for it have wandered away from the faith and pierced themselves [through and through] with many sorrows."
1 Timothy 6:10 (AMP)

QUOTE: "My favorite things in life don't cost any money. It's really clear that the most precious resource we all have is time." Steve Jobs

DISCUSSION: Do you own your money or does your money own you? Did your perspective on money change when you became an adult?

PRAYER: Open for prayer requests.

© 2017 National Association of Christian Women Entrepreneurs * All Rights Reserved * www.nacwe.org

Welcome to the weekly Prayer Call of

THE NATIONAL ASSOCIATION OF CHRISTIAN WOMEN ENTREPRENEURS ©

Our Mission
TO TRAIN, EMPOWER, AND INSPIRE CHRISTIAN WOMEN AS THEY BUILD THEIR ENTREPRENEURIAL BUSINESS/MINISTRY.

We do this in three ways: connect, create, and collaborate. We connect through the private forum, tele-classes, webinars, live events, and virtual events. We create through the power of idea sharing, resources, and vision. We collaborate by working with each other, creating joint ventures, sharing referrals, and walking side by side.

NACWE has always been known for its heart and we want to formally introduce you to our prayer and devotion corner, the Soul of NACWE. Our sisterhood is here to support you on your personal journey of faith and how that is intertwined with your business. We believe in the transformational power of prayer.
In our businesses, God is our CEO. http://nacwe.org/devotion

A CULTURE of GRATEFULNESS – November 23, 2017

Oh give thanks to the LORD, for He is good; for His steadfast love endures forever! Psalm 118:1-29 ESV

Every good gift and every perfect gift is from above, coming down from the Father of lights with whom there is no variation or shadow due to change. James 1:17 ESV

Do not be anxious about anything, but in everything by prayer and supplication with thanksgiving let your requests be made known to God. And the peace of God, which surpasses all understanding, will guard your hearts and your minds in Christ Jesus. Philippians 4:6-7 ESV

"He is a wise man who does not grieve for the things which he has not, but rejoices for those which he has." *Epictetus*

List some things for which you are grateful to God as a Christian, as a Woman; as an Entrepreneur in business/ministry.

What do you need to give to God in prayer and supplication to change anxiety into confidence? How do you make your requests known to Him *with thanksgiving?*

Can you offer a testimony of God's goodness and how gratefulness changed your life?

Copyright © National Association of Christian Women Entrepreneurs (NACWE) (2010-2017)
*All Rights Reserved. http://nacwe.org & http://www.facebook.com/NACWE/

Welcome to the weekly Prayer Call of

THE NATIONAL ASSOCIATION OF CHRISTIAN WOMEN ENTREPRENEURS ©

Our Mission
TO TRAIN, EMPOWER, AND INSPIRE CHRISTIAN WOMEN AS THEY BUILD THEIR ENTREPRENEURIAL BUSINESS/MINISTRY.

We do this in three ways: connect, create, and collaborate. We connect through the private forum, tele-classes, webinars, live events, and virtual events. We create through the power of idea sharing, resources, and vision. We collaborate by working with each other, creating joint ventures, sharing referrals, and walking side by side.

NACWE has always been known for its heart and we want to formally introduce you to our prayer and devotion corner, the Soul of NACWE. Our sisterhood is here to support you on your personal journey of faith and how that is intertwined with your business. We believe in the transformational power of prayer. **In our businesses, God is our CEO.** http://nacwe.org/devotion

A CULTURE of STEWARDSHIP – November 30, 2017

"Every good gift and every perfect gift is from above, coming down from the Father of lights with whom there is no variation or shadow due to change." James 1:17

"Do not lay up for yourselves treasures on earth, where moth and rust destroy and where thieves break in and steal, but lay up for yourselves treasures in heaven, where neither moth nor rust destroys and where thieves do not break in and steal. For where your treasure is, there your heart will be also." Matthew 6:19-21

"As each has received a gift, use it to serve one another, as good stewards of God's varied grace..." 1 Peter 4:10

Givers can be ..."like a honeycomb - which just overflows with its own sweetness. That is how God gives to us, and it is how we should give in turn." - **Anonymous**
We must recognize where everything we have comes from – It comes from the Lord! ASK:

In expending this, am I acting according to my character? Am I acting herein, not as a proprietor, but as a steward of my Lord's goods?
Am I doing this in obedience to his Word? In what Scripture does he require me so to do?
Can I offer up this action, this expense, as a sacrifice to God through Jesus Christ?...

Copyright © National Association of Christian Women Entrepreneurs (NACWE) (2010-2017)
*All Rights Reserved. http://nacwe.org & http://www.facebook.com/NACWE/

Prayer & Devotion

Celebrate Jesus, Celebrate You

DECEMBER 7, 2017

"For God so loved the world, that he gave his only Son, that whoever believes in him should not perish but have eternal life. John 3:16

For to us a child is born, to us a son is given; and the government shall be upon his shoulder, and his name shall be called Wonderful Counselor, Mighty God, Everlasting Father, Prince of Peace. Isaiah 9:6

And the Word became flesh and dwelt among us, and we have seen his glory, glory as of the only Son from the Father, full of grace and truth. John 1:14

Advent is the celebration of the arrival of a notable person. Is there anyone more notable that Jesus? What makes Jesus so notable? In what ways to do celebrate His notability during advent?

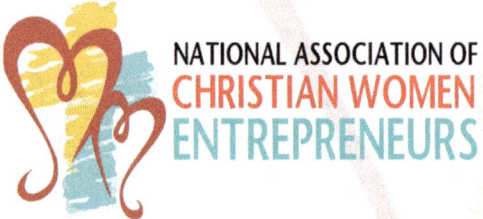

TO TRAIN, EMPOWER, AND INSPIRE CHRISTIAN WOMEN AS THEY BUILD THEIR ENTREPRENEURIAL BUSINESS/MINISTRY.

We do this in three ways: connect, create, and collaborate. We connect through the private forum, teleclasses, webinars, live events, and virtual events. We create through the power of idea sharing, resources, and vision. We collaborate by working with each other, creating joint ventures, sharing referrals, and walking side by side.

NACWE has always been known for its heart and we want to formally introduce you to our prayer and devotion corner, the Soul of NACWE. Our sisterhood is here to support you on your personal journey of faith and how that is intertwined with your business. We believe in the transformational power of prayer. In our businesses, God is our CEO. http://nacwe.org/devotion

Copyright © National Association of Christian Women Entrepreneurs (NACWE) (2010-2017)
*All Rights Reserved. http://nacwe.org & http://www.facebook.com/NACWE/

PRAYER & DEVOTION
Celebrate Jesus, Celebrate You

December 14, 2017

REJOICE - the act of spinning about, jumping around to the point of levity

"For outlandish creatures like us, on our way to a heart, a brain, and courage, Bethlehem is not the end of our journey but only the beginning - not home but the place through which we must pass if ever we are to reach home at last."
Frederick Buechner, The Magnificent Defeat

You who bring good news to Zion, go up on a high mountain. You who bring good news to Jerusalem, lift up your voice with a shout, lift it up, do not be afraid; say to the towns of Judah, "Here is your God!" See, the Sovereign LORD comes with power, and He rules with a mighty arm. See, his reward is with him, and his recompense accompanies him. He tends his flock like a shepherd: He gathers the lambs in his arms and carries them close to his heart; he gently leads those that have young. Isaiah 40:9-11

How beautiful on the mountains are the feet of the messenger who brings good news,
the good news of peace and salvation, the news that the God of Israel reigns! The watchmen shout and sing with joy, for before their very eyes they see the Lord returning to Jerusalem. Let the ruins of Jerusalem break into joyful song, for the Lord has comforted his people. He has redeemed Jerusalem. Isaiah 52:7-9

He came into the very world he created, but the world didn't recognize him. He came to his own people, and even they rejected him. But to all who believed him and accepted him, he gave the right to become children of God. John 1:10-12

How have you rejoiced at the coming of the King? Did you know you are the one He gave the right to become children of God? In what ways have you experienced the longing of waiting in comparison the the joy of His arrival?

PRAYER & DEVOTION
Celebrate Jesus, Celebrate You

December 21, 2017

HOPE - To trust in, wait for, look for, or desire something or someone; or to expect something beneficial in the future.

"Hope is the thing with feathers
That perches in the soul
And sings the tune without the words
And never stops at all."
— Emily Dickinson

But if we hope for what we do not see, we wait for it with patience. Romans 8:25

So that by two unchangeable things, in which it is impossible for God to lie, we who have fled for refuge might have strong encouragement to hold fast to the hope set before us. We have this as a sure and steadfast anchor of the soul, a hope that enters into the inner place behind the curtain, where Jesus has gone as a forerunner on our behalf, having become a high priest forever after the order of Melchizedek. Hebrews 6:18-20

"The Lord is my portion," says my soul, "therefore I will hope in him." Lamentations 3:24

But I will hope continually and will praise you yet more and more. Psalm 71:14

4,000 years passed from the time of the last prophet to the arrival of Jesus. 4,000 years of waiting. 4,000 years of holding onto hope. What have you hoped for so long you need supernatural strength to do it? What kind of things do you do to maintain hope for long periods of time? What thing have you hoped for that you finally got to see?

PRAYER & DEVOTION
Celebrate Jesus, Celebrate You

December 28, 2017

SALVATION & RESCUE

Saving us is the greatest and most concrete demonstration of God's love, the definitive display of His grace throughout time and eternity. -- David Jeremiah

Lead me in your truth and teach me, for you are the God of my salvation; for you, I wait all the day long. Psalm 25:5

But I with the voice of thanksgiving will sacrifice to you; what I have vowed I will pay. Salvation belongs to the Lord!" Jonah 2:9

My soul also is greatly troubled. But you, O Lord—how long? Turn, O Lord, deliver my life; save me for the sake of your steadfast love. Psalm 6:3-4

Jesus is born! The rescuer has arrived. What are you grateful to be rescued from? Is there anything you have vowed to do for the Lord, as Jonah did? Where have you seen the steadfast faithfulness of God's love in your life?

www.ingramcontent.com/pod-product-compliance
Lightning Source LLC
Chambersburg PA
CBHW060458300426
44113CB00016B/2635